BRITAIN IN OLD PHOTOGRAPHS

THE LONDON BOROUGH OF
ENFIELD

ALAN DUMAYNE

SUTTON PUBLISHING LIMITED

Sutton Publishing Limited
Phoenix Mill · Far Thrupp · Stroud
Gloucestershire · GL5 2BU

First published 1996
Reprinted 1996
Copyright © Alan Dumayne, 1996

British Library Cataloguing in Publication Data
A catalogue record for this book is available from the
British Library.

ISBN 0-7509-1027-5

Typeset in 10/12 Perpetua.
Typesetting and origination by
Sutton Publishing Limited.
Printed in Great Britain by
Ebenezer Baylis, Worcester.

This book would not have been possible without the assistance of Graham Dalling, Local
History Officer for the London Borough of Enfield, whose wide knowledge on local
matters has provided inspiration whenever needed. I am most grateful to him and to his
assistants, Kate and Maureen. My thanks also to the Local Authority for allowing me to
delve into their files to select so many photographs from a past era and for allowing their
reproduction in this book. It has proved a daunting but most pleasurable task.

Alan Dumayne

The Market Square, Enfield, 1897.

CONTENTS

Introduction   5

1. Out in the Country   7

2. Forty Hill and Bulls Cross   15

3. Enfield Town   25

4. Around the Town   37

5. Bush Hill Park   47

6. Eastern Enfield   55

7. Ponders End   63

8. River Lea   71

9. Lower Edmonton   77

10. Upper Edmonton   87

11. Southgate and New Southgate   95

12. Palmers Green   107

13. Winchmore Hill   119

14. Transport   131

15. Wartime   145

    Index   158

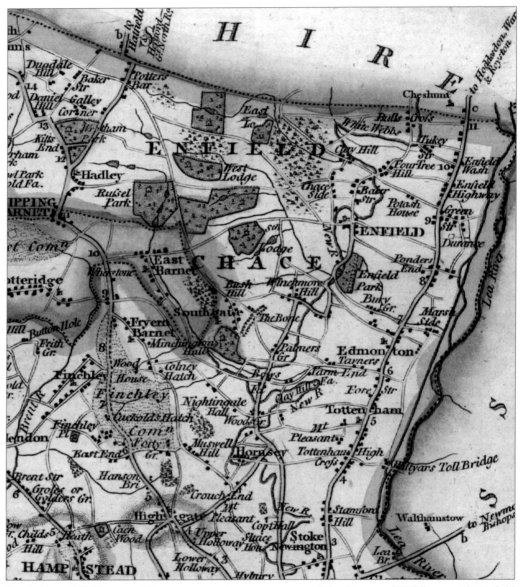

Cary's Map of 1793 shows this extreme north-eastern corner of the County of Middlesex with 'Enfield Chace' prominent. Originally part of an even larger estate, Enfield Chase became Crown land in 1421 and remained in Royal hands for more than 350 years. Densely forested, and a favourite hunting ground for Royal parties, the Chase totalled over 8,300 acres and stretched northwards as far as Potters Bar. It was disafforested in 1777, when it was divided up between the King and various freeholders.

INTRODUCTION

The London Borough of Enfield, which came into being in 1965, constitutes a very large area totalling more than twenty thousand acres and is comprised of many diverse regions, each with a different background and history. Strict editing has been required, therefore, in preparing this volume and apologies are offered for the unavoidable omissions.

In early times, a huge forest extended across outer London, north of the Thames. Evidence has been uncovered of Roman settlements in the area, and of the roads they built to serve the city.

In Saxon times, more clearings were made and small hamlets grew up at several vantage points in the region. One such was at Southgate (recorded as Suthgate in 1371, which was then within the parish of Edmonton). The name was derived from the spot where five tracks met at the South Gate into Enfield Chase. Southgate was historically part of the parish of Edmonton, and it was not until 1881 that it gained its independence. The name Edmonton is Saxon in origin and is thought to be derived from 'Eadhelmes tun', the village of Eadhelm, a leading Saxon noble.

Enfield, at this time, consisted of a number of small hamlets, and formed part of the Hundred of Edmonton. The origin of the name Enfield is thought to be Saxon, field being felled, or a clearing in the forest belonging to Eana. The term 'Hundred' has little relevance today. It was created originally as the amalgamation of ten tithings. In turn, a tithing consisted of a group of ten freeholders, working side by side. Thus the Hundred comprised, in total, one hundred freeholders and their families.

In Norman times, there was a marked increase in the number of manors recorded within the region, and most of the large landowners of this period, now just names to us, can also be determined.

Between 1609 and 1613, Sir Hugh Myddelton was busy with his successful project of creating the New River, designed to bring fresh, clean water into the capital from the springs of Hertfordshire. Much of its course flows through the region and, during this period, Sir Hugh lived in a big house at the top of Bush Hill, which later became Halliwick, recently demolished. The 'river' – in truth a canal – was a project years ahead of its time and of great credit to its creators.

In 1610, Sir John Weld came to live at 'Arnolds' in Southgate and was dismayed to find that the villagers faced a long walk in order to worship at All Saints in Edmonton. To remedy this situation, he built the Weld Chapel in Waterfall Lane in 1615 which subsequently, thanks to the benefaction of the Walker family, gave way to Christ Church in 1862.

The Quakers, too, had an early presence in the area, with Meeting Houses in both Winchmore Hill and Enfield, from as early as 1688 and 1697 respectively.

In 1619, a new Charter by James I confirmed Enfield's right to hold a weekly market and, in 1629, Sir Nicholas Raynton built Forty Hall. The Parish Church of Enfield, situated behind the Market Square, is dedicated to St Andrew, and is of very ancient origin. Parts of the existing edifice are thought to date from the twelfth century, but its history goes back to pre-Norman times.

The densely forested Enfield Chase, totalling 8,300 acres and extending as far north as Potters Bar, was a happy hunting ground for Royal parties and, with the disafforestation in 1777, it gave rise to a further influx of eminent and affluent personages, intent on setting up their stately homes in such ideal surroundings.

There followed a period of steady growth, but the scene remained largely rural, with farming the chief occupation of the villagers.

As the nineteenth century came to a close, however, there was a marked acceleration in growth. The railways had arrived and some of the big landowners were selling. These included the Taylors of Grovelands and the Walkers of Arnos Grove. Development ensued at different rates within the region. This was as evident then as it is today, with the tremendous variety of scenes we have within the London Borough of Enfield.

The trams, buses and the Tube all played major roles as the rapid expansion continued. The creation of suburbia was interesting to witness as roads and houses were soon to be followed by the churches, schools, shops and places of entertainment. It all happened in such a short space of time.

This century has seen many changes, both in our local and in our social history, and the pace still quickens. Since the Second World War there has been an inflow of residents from other parts of the globe, settling here to become part of the local community.

Enfield's industry, once so active on the eastern side of the borough, has gone into considerable decline, as well-established companies have been taken over, moved elsewhere or simply yielded to foreign competition. The local shops, once our pride and joy, have struggled to survive the competition of the new supermarkets and the shopping centres. This, of course, is not just a local phenomenon, but one of much wider context.

This likewise applies to the massive increase in the traffic on our roads, leading to congestion, pollution and the necessary creation of large car parking facilities. Such is the price of progress!

OUT IN
THE COUNTRY

There will be many references to farming in the pages that follow, and here we see haymaking in progress in the fields near Clay Hill, c. 1890.

A rural scene in Whitewebbs: a former country pathway, no longer existent, leads through the woods towards the King and Tinker in Whitewebbs Lane.

A pleasant walk at the top of Hilly Fields leads us down Cooks Hole Road to the Thatched Cottage, one of the few remaining thatched roof dwellings in the region. 'The Hermitage' in Cannon Hill is another example.

Phipps Hatch Lane, looking west, with Hilly Fields to the right and what is now Gloucester Road on the left. The scene is much changed now but Hilly Fields, made a public park in 1911, is a haven of peace and many of the mature trees remain.

Chase Farm on The Ridgeway was built in 1886 as a Poor Law Orphanage. In the 1930s the establishment was run down and, by 1938, it was being used to house old people. It became a hospital in 1939 and, though the main building has changed little, the building programme continues with new wards replacing the old.

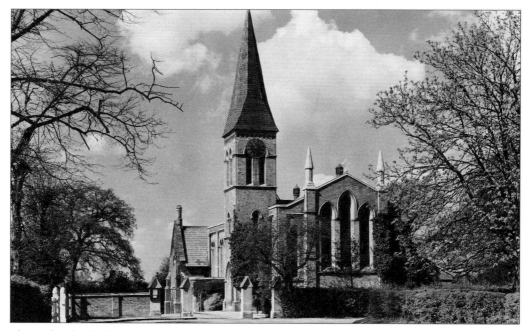

Christ Church, Chalk Lane, Cockfosters was built in 1839 by Robert Bevan of West Farm Place and Trent Park. The Bevan family, wealthy bankers, had close and very long standing connections with the Cockfosters area.

The Rose and Crown in Clay Hill, once the centre of a tiny hamlet called Bridge Street. One of the very old inns of Enfield, situated in the hollow between Hilly Fields and Whitewebbs Park, it still retains a country outlook. Mr Nott, Dick Turpin's grandfather, is reputed to have been the licensee here in the early years of the eighteenth century.

The King and Tinker, thought to be one of the oldest inns in Enfield. Legend has it that King James I was staying at Theobalds and, whilst hunting in the forest, became detached from his nobles. He stopped at a small alehouse and got into conversation with an unsuspecting tinker. A delightful old ballad tells the story more fully.

Halfway along The Ridgeway, at the junction of East Lodge Lane, lies the hamlet of Botany Bay which includes a pub, a farm, a garage (car repairs), a small chapel and a cricket club. The origin of the name remains a mystery, though there are several unproven theories.

In 1777, Dr Richard Jebb, physician to the royal household, hurried out to Trento in the Austrian Tyrol to successfully treat a very sick Duke of Gloucester. A delighted George III awarded him this portion of Enfield Chase. Trent Park has seen many changes in its history, in which the Bevan and Sassoon families figure prominently, and it is now part of the Middlesex University.

This grand mid-nineteenth-century family home in Clay Hill had a lovely setting close by Hilly Fields and must have witnessed some marvellous times in days gone by.

St John's Church, built in 1857, was designed by James Piers St Aubyn. Of attractive appearance, it features bi-coloured brick window heads and string courses. The church is situated in Clay Hill, opposite the Fallow Buck, where the area still retains a rural atmosphere.

Beech Hill Park is now the clubhouse of Hadley Wood Golf Club, which opened in 1922. In the early 1880s Charles Jack, who owned the mansion and much of the land, drew up plans to develop the Hadley Wood area. It resulted in the opening of the station in 1885 and subsequent development.

The M25, which lies on the extreme northern borders of the borough, has had a profound effect on the many roads feeding into it. In August 1979, the Mayor of Enfield, Councillor Graham Eustance, surveys construction work on the new motorway, just to the north of Crews Hill. Burnt Farm Ride in the middle of the picture crosses what had been dense woodland.

FORTY HILL
AND BULLS CROSS

The view from Forty Hall across the lake is timeless and much enjoyed by local residents. Sadly, the avenue of limes, seen here, was severely depleted during the hurricane of October 1987.

At the southern end of Forty Hill, overlooking the green, stands The Hermitage, dating from 1704. It became a veterinary surgeon's premises for a time and, in 1927, the pond was filled in.

The Goat, seen here c. 1910, now serves as a private residence, but the 'new' pub on the island site nearby remains the hub of a small community, with a post office and a few shops clustered around. Today's mixture of old and new buildings still manages to retain a village-style atmosphere.

In spite of local pleas to preserve the Old Bakery, this delightful old weather-boarded building was demolished in March 1968. It was situated at the extreme southern end of Forty Hill, where the road is now blocked off to through-traffic.

Worcester Lodge, from a painting by John Hill, who lived on the premises and died in 1841. Situated on the south side of Goat Lane, the fine proportions of this house can still be appreciated. It once served as the manse for what was then the chapel in Baker Street.

Jesus Church, near to Maidens Bridge, was built in 1835 as a chapel of ease to St Andrew's but, in 1845, it became a parish church in its own right. The building was endowed by Christian Paul Meyer of Forty Hall and had close connections with E.A. 'Gussie' Bowles of Myddelton House.

The village smithy was never short of work in an age when horses played such an important role in our lives. Mr Elston was the official farrier to Colonel Sir Alfred Somerset's famous hunt. The smithy survived until 1931.

The small hamlet of Bulls Cross could once boast of two inns in close proximity. The Pied Bull still trades, but this former country pub, The Spotted Cow, with post office attached, stopped serving customers in 1924. It has reverted to private ownership and is now known as 'The Orchards'.

Looking across the lake to Forty Hall. This fine Jacobean mansion was built between 1629 and 1632 for Sir Nicholas Raynton, Lord Mayor of London, in the grounds of an earlier mansion, Elsynge Hall. Forty Hall was purchased by Henry C.B. Bowles in 1895 and it remained the family home until 1951.

Forty Hall, south elevation. Now taken over by the Local Authority and set in lovely surroundings, the mansion is very much a focal point for residents. It houses a museum, art gallery, exhibition rooms, a banqueting suite and a popular café.

The design of Forty Hall is sometimes attributed to Inigo Jones, though this is uncertain. His influence is evident here, in this grand and stately archway leading to the stable courtyard.

Forty Hall, interior. The richness of the beautiful cornices and mural decorations can still be appreciated. This fine plasterwork, seen here in the entrance hall, was executed *c.* 1787.

This portrait of Sir Nicholas Raynton, which was painted when he was seventy-four, hangs above the fireplace in 'The Raynton Room' on the ground floor and is thought to be the work of William Dobson. Sir Nicholas died in 1646.

Maidens Bridge crosses Turkey Brook, where Forty Hill meets Bulls Cross. Parts of the bridge date from 1761, but major repairs to the superstructure were needed in 1968, following damage by a lorry. The narrowness of the bridge demands a single-flow system controlled by traffic lights, but the scene remains pleasantly rural.

Capel Manor was built in the mid- or late eighteenth century, near the site of Honeylands Manor House. The last private owner was Lt.-Col. Sydney Medcalf, a noted breeder of Clydesdale horses, who died in 1958. The house and grounds now serve as a college, specializing in horticultural and environmental education.

ENFIELD TOWN

Workmen busy in Enfield Town on the final stages of the tramway. On 1 July 1909, amidst much celebration, the first tramcar, with many dignitaries on board, progressed from The Green Dragon to the new terminus, The George Inn. The extension from Manor House was now complete.

The Queens Hall cinema in London Road was considered luxurious when it opened in 1911. With the coming of the 'talkies', a balcony was added and the capacity almost doubled. It was closed after damage during the Second World War, but reopened in 1947 as the Florida. It finally closed in 1976 and was later converted into The Townhouse.

In succession to the old Vestry House in Church Street, this 'new' police station was built in 1872, on the corner of London Road and Cecil Road. It has since been demolished and replaced by a modern station, in Baker Street.

Enfield, a quiet market town in the late nineteenth century, looking west down Church Street. The large three-storey building is the Greyhound Inn, which ceased to function after 1860. It was eventually demolished to make way for today's even larger and grander bank premises.

The Vestry House was erected to serve as a beadle's office with a 'cage' each side for miscreants. The Metropolitan Police took it over in 1840 until the new station was built in London Road in 1872. This historic building now serves as solicitors' offices.

The Fountain, looking north towards Silver Street, *c.* 1905. On traffic-free roads, two horses pause for refreshment at the drinking trough. The Nags Head pub, right of picture, had been rebuilt in 1882 to effectively widen the entry into Southbury Road.

The Town, looking east, *c.* 1929. Mechanical transport has replaced the horse with motor cars, vans and a tram in evidence, but no yellow lines. Facing us is the Nags Head and Southbury Road, once called Nags Head Lane.

Looking west down Church Street, with the Fountain in the foreground. A quiet scene at the turn of the century. Ebben's Steam Bakery and the George Inn feature on the left, and a tree-lined pavement on the right leads to the imposing 'new' bank building.

The matchboarded front of Ebben's Steam Bakery can be clearly seen, with the George set back from the road. Next to the inn is an imposing five-storey building dating from 1897. It was once the home of James Meyers' subscription library and local newspaper interests. Beyond is Enfield House and Pearson's premises.

This picture records a family outing from the George, with time for a leisurely spin around the town, in the days before the motor car.

View from the church tower, looking south across the market square. The cedar tree, which stood in the Palace grounds, dominates the skyline. A plaque in today's shopping precinct commemorates this tree which stood here until 1929. It is thought to have been the first Cedar of Lebanon in this country, planted by Dr Robert Uvedale in 1663.

A very quiet late nineteenth-century scene of the market square, showing the Kings Head and St Andrew's Church. The old market cross, seen here, has found its final resting place in the garden of Myddelton House, since being replaced by the market house in 1904.

The market traders begin to set out their stalls. This photograph was taken soon after the erection of the market house in 1904, an octagonal structure supported on eight columns of teak with an inscription on the fascia, commemorating the coronation of Edward VII.

When the Palace site was auctioned in 1918, Lot No. 1 comprised these two old shops, facing on to the market square. The purchaser was Pearsons, whose premises adjoined. P. & H. Watts moved to Genotin Road where the hairdressing business still operates.

Enfield's market has long been established. In 1303, the Lord of the Manor was granted a licence to hold a weekly market and two annual fairs. In 1619, the market was granted a charter by James I. The fairs were discontinued in the late 1800s, but the stallholders, seen here in 1979, are as busy as ever.

A lovely old scene in Church Street, looking west, showing some of the old shops and the Rising Sun, demolished in the early 1930s to allow for road widening. The Highways Department is busy here, carrying out minor repairs to the roadway.

Church Street, looking west, *c*. 1900. On the left we see a parade of shops with the Rising Sun in the far distance. On the right, a brick wall guards Burleigh House, a fine mansion finally vacated in 1912 and demolished the following year.

Messrs Coote, builder and undertaker, stood near to the corner with Cecil Road. In olden times, the builder performed many tasks. His joiners were skilled at making coffins and, with transport available, a full funeral service could be offered.

Church Street, looking east, *c.* 1906. As Enfield's population grew, so the town needed a new and larger purpose-built post office. These premises opened in Church Street in 1906.

A new and beautifully tiled Sainsbury's shop opened in Church Street in 1898. Its appeal was immediate and business was good (see next page). Henry Webb, delivery lad, poses for the camera in 1913.

Sainsbury's new shop in Church Street, *c.* 1901. Butchers were proud of their open-air displays of meat and poultry, especially during the period leading up to Christmas. One wonders what today's Public Health Inspector would think of such displays.

AROUND THE TOWN

The Public Offices, a stately Georgian building at No. 1 Gentleman's Row, was once a private residence set in extensive grounds. Originally known as Little Park, it came under the control of the Local Authority in 1888. It has served many purposes since, including housing the Local Registrar's Office.

The Church of St Mary Magdalene was erected in 1883 and is a landmark for miles around. The windmill, seen here, was erected in the early 1800s, replacing former windmills dating back to the early sixteenth century, and was finally demolished in 1904.

The Bycullah Athenaeum in Windmill Hill opened in 1883 to much acclaim. It had a chequered history, featuring concerts, plays, films, dances, election counts and many other functions, until its final demise in December 1931, when it was destroyed by fire. The site is now occupied by the Old Oak Motor Company.

Old Park Avenue. This rural scene reminds us of years gone by and the lovely walk that led eventually to Winchmore Hill. Amidst the most beautiful countryside, walkers passed Pike's Farm, crossed Salmon's Brook and picked their way through the orchards to emerge into a very leafy Green Dragon Lane.

The famous essayist, Charles Lamb, and his sister Mary moved into Chase Side in 1827. Charles often expressed delight with his new home and lifestyle, away from 'wicked' London. Sometimes he was in sombre, less complimentary mood, no doubt affected by Mary's health problems.

Gentleman's Row, so near to the bustle of town, remains a quiet backwater, with elegant buildings of the seventeenth and eighteenth centuries looking across to gardens by the banks of the New River. Charles and Mary Lamb originally boarded at Clarendon Cottage, seen here (stucco front, middle distance).

Chase Side, looking north, with Christ Church in the distance. Stribling's grocer's shop is trading on the corner with Chase Green Avenue, and there is a general air of peaceful calm.

Looking east from Chase Side down a very narrow Parsonage Lane, with Wood House and Ivy House facing the pond. They were both demolished in 1905, and the pond filled in the following year, allowing the lane to be widened.

Ivy Cottage stood in Chase Side, almost opposite Trinity Street, prior to its demolition about 1930. This shows the typical clapboarded construction with dormer windows featured in the roof.

A tree-lined Silver Street, looking south towards London Road. We witness a peaceful town centre with Grout's, the saddler's, on the corner of Southbury Road; the site is now occupied by Lloyds Bank, built in 1892. Opposite, with corner turret, stands the newly appointed Nags Head, built in 1882.

Silver Street, looking north, *c.* 1900. The corner of Church Lane can just be seen on the left, and the area in the middle distance on the right is now occupied by the Civic Centre.

The Jolly Farmers in Slades Hill. This delightful little beerhouse bears no resemblance to the large modern pub, built in 1935, that has replaced it, though McMullen's Ales are still available. This spot was once known as Frogs Bottom, where Salmons Brook washed over a country lane.

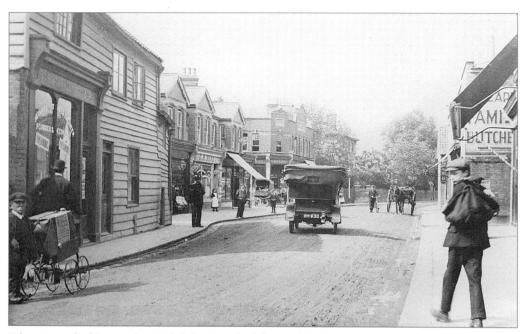

Baker Street, looking north with Bell Road on the left in middle distance, *c.* 1914. The corner shop, built in 1900, has become Enterprise House, commercial offices. The clapboarded shops in foreground have since been demolished to allow for road widening and straightening.

The Hop Poles stands at the junction of Lancaster Road and Baker Street. This old inn, pictured here in 1890, was demolished in 1909 and replaced by a more modern building. Opposite once stood the Canon Brewery.

Enfield Court in Baker Street was once the home of Colonel Sir Alfred Somerset, a noted Enfield dignitary, a fine horseman and Master of the Enfield Chase Staghounds. The house was built around 1690, enlarged in 1864 and, following the death of Lady Somerset, it became a school in 1925.

Baker Street, looking north. In the distance is Gough Park, home of Richard Gough, an eighteenth-century antiquarian. The house was demolished at the turn of the century, but a gate and some railings survive to remind us of past glories.

In 1965, the boroughs of Southgate and Edmonton lost their independence and, together with Enfield, a new London Borough of Enfield was formed. On 6 May 1975, Her Majesty, Queen Elizabeth the Queen Mother, officially opened the new tower block of the Civic Centre in Silver Street.

BUSH HILL PARK

Queen Anne's Gardens was once the home of Bush Hill Park Golf Club. The Club was obliged to leave the course by Christmas 1911, when the land was sold for development.

The magnificent headquarters of the Bush Hill Park Golf Club today. The Club started in 1895, but in 1911–12 it leased 108 acres of the Old Park estate and laid out a new course. The last private owner of the estate was John Walker Ford.

Bush Hill House was the home of Sir Hugh Myddelton during the time he was masterminding the construction of the New River (1609–13). Much altered, the house later became Halliwick College, run by the Church of England Children's Society for disabled young people, but it was demolished in 1993 and replaced by blocks of flats.

Jews Corner, a much photographed beauty spot. Today's Ridge Road was once known as Jews Corner Lane and, where the lane met Church Street, it was always known as Jews Corner. The origins of the name remain shrouded in mystery.

This quaint old bridge crossed Salmons Brook and led to Montefiore Place, Little Bury Street, where this row of eighteenth-century cottages survived into the 1930s. The bridge has been rebuilt and modern housing has replaced the cottages.

Even the washing line fails to diminish the charm of this old cottage, once situated on the west side of Little Bury Street.

The Heath family were prominent nurserymen operating in Barrowell Green, Palmers Green (at Chequers Keep and The Elms), Firs Lane and here at the Ramscroft Nursery in Bury Street. The whole area was once rich in nurseries, which have gradually succumbed to development.

This imposing Jacobean house, Bury Hall, was situated on the south side of Bury Street, very close to where the busy A10 now crosses. The last private owner was William Bowater of papermaking fame, prior to demolition in 1920 to make way for the road. A once rural scene has been replaced by the constant roar of traffic.

Bedroom ceiling detail in one of the rooms of Bury Hall. This example indicates clearly the tremendous skills of the designer and the plasterer.

The Stag and Hounds, Bury Street West, *c.* 1910. Once set in open farmland and nursery gardens, and a regular meeting place for the 'Stag Hounds', this lovely old inn was demolished in 1925 and rebuilt further back to allow for road widening.

This cottage once stood at the junction of Bury Street and Little Bury Street, nearly opposite The Stag and Hounds. It was demolished when the road was straightened and widened prior to development.

Salisbury House, one of the oldest survivors, is situated on the south side of Bury Street West, adjoining Bury Lodge Park, a bowls club and a nursery. The house has seen mixed fortunes during its lifetime. It was once owned by the Pratley family, local nurserymen in this area.

Salisbury House, east elevation. Purchased by the Edmonton authorities in the 1930s, the house became an arts centre in 1957 and, now much restored, is a popular meeting place for many local societies.

St Stephen's 'Iron Church' opened in 1901 and was set in open and quiet rural surroundings. When the new church was built, it continued to serve as the Church Hall until 1925, when it was demolished to make way for the much grander hall we have today.

A familiar view of St Stephen's Church, showing a tram and a motor car on their way to Enfield, c. 1928. The 'new' church and the 'new' hall (behind tram) can be seen, together with the lychgate, on the corner of Village Road. This was unveiled in 1922 and serves also as a war memorial.

EASTERN ENFIELD

Enfield Lock, showing the entrance to the Royal Small Arms Factory which, particularly in times of crisis, became a huge employer of local labour.

The Royal Small Arms Factory covered a huge site at Enfield Lock, beginning production in 1816. The power required was originally derived from waterwheels driven by the River Lea, and both raw materials coming in and finished products leaving the factory were transported by barge.

The Boer War peace treaty was signed on 31 May 1902. Although it could pose a threat to their jobs, it was time for the 'lockies' (workers) to celebrate. Note the tradition of foremen in bowlers and workers in cloth caps.

On the extreme eastern borders of the borough, running north to south, is the River Lea; several water courses join it in its flow southwards into the Thames. This area was marshland near Enfield Lock.

Government Row, on the banks of the River Lea Navigation, provided housing for the 'lockies' of the RSA Factory. Flooding was always a threat during the wet winter months.

The laying of the foundation stone of a new church dedicated to St Peter and St Paul, which opened in Ordnance Road in May 1928. The church was wrecked in 1944 by a V1 but has since been rebuilt.

Hertford Road, Enfield Wash, looking south, c. 1905. Prospect House, the pub on left built in 1899, is now occupied by Barclays Bank. The Prince of Wales, in the middle distance on the right, survives. At the turn of the century, horses were still fully employed before the age of the motor.

On the north side of Turkey Street some of the footbridges over the brook have gone, as have some of the old houses they served. The brook still runs, however, and the area still bears a certain charm of yesteryear.

The brook in Turkey Street, looking east, *c.* 1968. This footbridge and the lamp-posts still survive. The footpath wends its way on the left and the white stucco building, on the opposite bank, is The Turkey pub.

Engraving of Enfield Wash, from a book dated 1809. The book describes Enfield Wash as 'a stream which takes its rise in Enfield Chase and proceeds to the River Lea. In the winter it becomes a rapid stream and urges its waves across the high road to the danger of carriages and passengers.'

St James' Church, Hertford Road, Enfield Highway, was built in 1831 and suffered serious fire damage in 1967. The east end has been rebuilt in modified form. The churchyard incorporates a large cemetery adjoining Durants Park.

Class at St George's School, Freezywater, 1930. The old school was set up in 1903, opposite Ordnance Road, but moved in 1936 to a new building behind the church. Does anyone, now in their seventies, recognize themselves or their classmates in this picture?

Enfield Wash, Hertford Road, looking north. The shop on the right, with sunblinds down, is on the corner of Albany Road, and the signpost on the pavement advertises the Prince of Wales pub opposite.

Lincoln Road, somewhere between Enfield and Ponders End. A tree-lined and leafy lane at the turn of the century reminds us of times past when the pace of life was so much slower.

Turkey Street, looking east towards Hertford Road, *c.* 1973. The brook flows under the Woolpack bridge. The Sun and Woolpack pub is on the opposite bank, but the high-rise flats remind us of more modern times.

PONDERS END

In this delightful photograph of 1909, we see The Two Brewers pub, built in 1896 on the corner of High Street and South Street. The German bombers ended its life in 1940 and the site remains undeveloped.

In 1809, Grout & Baylis' crape factory was built in South Street. It was fashionable in the nineteenth century to wear mourning for a long period following bereavement, and the workforce grew to two hundred. The demand dwindled, causing the factory to close in 1894.

The old crape factory was taken over by United Flexible Metal Tubing. Its products were originally designed for the gas industry but, adapting to other needs, the company prospered. The factory was demolished in 1991.

The High Road. The White Hart Inn still survives, just south of the junction with Nags Head Road, though deliveries are no longer made by horse and cart, and the trams are just a distant memory.

The Eeles' family forge survived for nearly two hundred years before being wrecked in the blitz of 1940. The photograph is dated 1910. The forge stood on the present site of the library and car park, north of Derby Road.

High Street, Ponders End at the turn of the century, before the arrival of the trams (1907) or the motor cars. The cyclists are quite safe to take up the centre of the roadway and London seemed a long way off.

South Street, seen here at the turn of the century, has changed almost beyond recognition. St Matthew's Church, two pubs and a few old dwellings survive but modern high-rise flats tower above the gas holders and the estate development bears no relation to the old.

The Ponders End Mill, latterly known as Wright's Mill. George Wright came to the area in 1864 to serve as manager and was subsequently taken into partnership, prior to his death in 1914. The family connection has been maintained and business remains buoyant.

The Hertford Road Post Office in June 1909 was a quite amazing 'emporium'. The newsagent's offered 'good accommodation for cyclists' and sold everything from sweets, tobacco and ice-cream to coal for the grate and buckets and spades for the beach.

The Ponders End & Enfield Highway Gas Company was formed in 1859 and the works in South Street opened in the following January. There was expansion in 1882, with the board constantly staving off their rivals, the electricity supply companies. The gasworks closed down in 1970.

The Ponders End Congregational Church Choir assemble for their annual outing, some time in the 1920s. The capacity of these early open 'charabancs' is clear, and there is not a seat belt in sight.

The Ponders End Picture Palace opened in 1913. It was far from palatial and admission was 3*d* and 6*d* for adults. Though its name changed over the years, it continued to serve into the 'talkies' era, until its closure with the outbreak of the Second World War.

The heydays of the cinema above are gone. Used as a store for aircraft parts during the war, it later became a dance hall and a community centre, known as Howard Hall, but its fortunes continued to fluctuate through some good and some very bad times.

RIVER LEA

A charming, pre-1914 view on the towpath of the River Lea, looking south from Ponders End Lock.

Barge traffic on the Lea, once an important lifeline into and out of the capital.

Ponders End Lock, looking north, with many signs of industry on the banks. The tall chimney spotlights the Ediswan factory, while the trusty steed is being given a rest from barge duties.

What a charming couple they make from a bygone era on the tumbling bay bridge at Enfield Lock, just to the north of the Royal Small Arms Factory.

Just to the south of the Angel Road bridge, the furniture factories are seen receiving supplies of timber, ready for milling and manufacture.

The familiar Lea Valley Viaduct, looking north, 1964. Spanning the River Lea Navigation, the viaduct is part of the ever-busy North Circular Road.

Enfield Lock, 1910. The operation of the lock gates continues to fascinate us all, as it has through the ages.

The Ha'penny Bridge, which was once part of a lovely walk that stretched from Edmonton across to Epping Forest. It disappeared with the construction of the William Girling reservoir.

This lock at Rammey Marsh lies just south of the M25 on the extreme north-eastern border of the borough. The electricity pylons seem out of place here.

The lock-keepers' houses have a distinctive style of their own. This photograph was taken at Picketts Lock in 1964.

LOWER EDMONTON

The Crosskeys at Edmonton Green, 1886. The footbridge crosses Salmon's Brook, and the track of the old low-level railway can just be seen.

These attractive Saddlers Mill Bridge cottages, demolished in 1906, stood on the eastern side of the Hertford Road, opposite Bury Street. The Saddlers Mill stream passes under the roadway.

Edmonton Green, east side, *c.* 1949. A few of the shops and a small section of the street market are shown before development. Linwood's was noted for its fresh fish.

East side of the Green, looking north towards Hertford Road, *c.* 1886. Young's, the baker's, is in the foreground and beyond is Beeton's butcher's shop. This scene has completely disappeared with the redevelopment.

The modern version of Edmonton Green, 1975. It features a large shopping centre and blocks of high-rise flats.

Ragg's pharmacy and post office stood next to the Crosskeys and served the public for over a century.

The Pioneer Cycle Company was established in Hertford Road in 1880, a boom time for cycles. Note the very early motor cars, dating from around 1905.

Fore Street, looking north, *c*. 1900. This scene has disappeared. The horsetrams were replaced by the electric-powered version around 1905. The Town Hall and the Congregational Church have been demolished since the Second World War.

Cook & Jones, pawnbrokers and general dealers, on the corner of Fore Street and Bridge Road, *c.* 1905. The pawnbroker once played a major part in many people's lives. The shop was a real emporium of riches. Note the clothing division on the extreme left of the picture.

Fore Street, looking north, *c.* 1906. Sebastopol Road is opposite. The arrival of the electrified tramway no doubt prompted this photograph.

All Saints Church. A church has existed on this site since at least the early twelfth century. This historic centre of worship, with churchyard attached, once had close ties with the Southgate area, before its own parish churches became established.

The grave of Charles Lamb (1775–1834) and his sister Mary (1764–1847) in All Saints churchyard. The Lambs first visited Enfield in 1825 and took up residence there in 1827, before moving to Edmonton in 1833.

The Lambs' cottage, Church Street. In May 1833, Charles and Mary left Enfield to take up residence here at the Waldens' home, where Mary had previously boarded during bouts of illness. At the end of the following year, Charles was taken ill; he died on 27 December 1834. The cottage still exists today.

A very early photograph of Church Street, looking west with the thatched roof cottages on the corner with Church Lane, *c.* 1865. Note the boundary wall of All Saints on the left and the trees, some of which still exist.

Compare this scene with the one above. The year is 1890. We see a better road surface, pavements and some street lighting, but the next picture reveals a more striking transformation.

The distinctive Charles Lamb Institute has replaced the cottages. Built in 1908 as the church hall for All Saints, it was disposed of in the 1970s to become the Tower Gym.

The Armistice of 1918 was followed by the Treaty of Versailles, signed on 28 June 1919 after lengthy negotiations. It prompted many celebratory 'Peace Teas', this one being held in Rosebery Road, just off Victoria Road.

UPPER EDMONTON

The Bell, 1820. The inn became a legend after the poem by William Cowper was published in 1782, about John Gilpin's famous ride from Cheapside. His runaway horse overshot the intended destination, the Edmonton Bell, and finished up in Ware, fourteen miles further on. The inn disappeared in the 1960s.

Just south of The Bell this pub, the White Horse, has survived, but has been extensively rebuilt. It stands on the corner of Fore Street and Colyton Way. All the shops have been rebuilt too, and the horses and carts replaced by a different form of traffic.

The junction of Silver Street and Fore Street will always be known as The Angel. It derives from an old tavern of that name that stood here for years. This pub is the Victorian version that gave way, in 1930, to a more modern building. In 1968, major road widening saw its final demise.

The scene depicted here, on the extreme southern borders of the borough, is unrecognizable today. The Congregational Church has been demolished in postwar years to make way for blocks of flats, and a large factory complex has replaced the cottages at the entry into Langhedge Lane.

Angel Cottages, Angel Road, Edmonton, alias Jack Straw's Dining Rooms, where a cut off the joint and two veg. would cost you sixpence (2½p). Those were the days!

The Alcazar Cinematograph Theatre opened in Fore Street on 28 June 1913. The arcade of Moorish design was a notable feature. It was an ambitious project, with a separate dance hall and the Winter and Summer Gardens, designed for public enjoyment. It was destroyed in the blitz of 1940 (see pp. 151–2).

The staff of the Alcazar assemble for a day's outing and once again the open 'chara' demonstrates its enormous capacity.

The familiar twin towers of the Lea Valley Viaduct, opened in 1927, are seen here, looking west towards Epping Forest.

These are the premises of Bennett Taff Ltd, furniture manufacturers, in 1933, indicating the industry of the region. The Lea Valley Viaduct can be seen in the distance.

Pymmes Park and House, *c*. 1890. In 1582 the house was purchased by William Cecil, Lord Burghley, and in 1589 his famous son, Robert Cecil, spent his honeymoon here. Pymmes Park officially opened in 1906, but the house was destroyed by fire in 1940.

A thanksgiving service being held in Pymmes Park on VJ Day, 15 August 1948, just three years after the surrender of Japan, which brought the Second World War to a close.

These shops once lay between Victoria Road, beyond which the entrance to Pymmes Park can be seen, and Silver Street Station. A once peaceful area has succumbed to roadworks and the constant traffic along the busy North Circular Road.

Silver Street, near the junction with Fore Street, where the road dips under the railway bridge, 1965. During prolonged heavy rainfall, this U-bend has tended to flood over the years.

The name Weir Hall Gardens reminds us of past splendour. The original Wyer Hall lay slightly to the north but Mr Sage, a wealthy shopfitter, built Weir Hall in 1870, set in idyllic grounds. Amidst fluctuating fortunes, it once thrived as a reputable college prior to demolition in 1934, to make way for housing.

In 1914, the Board of Guardians for the Edmonton Union Workhouse Infirmary offered the War Office 150 beds for the treatment of wounded soldiers. The Ministry of Health took over in 1920 and renamed it the North Middlesex Hospital, now one of North London's main general hospitals.

SOUTHGATE AND NEW SOUTHGATE

Southgate's smithy served the community for three hundred years, until 1932 saw its demise with the coming of the Tube.

Bunker's Corner in the 1880s. The long-established wheelwright's and ironworker's premises were demolished in 1897, to make way for some 'new' shops, but this is now the site of Southgate Tube Station.

1933 saw the arrival of the Tube and the formation of Southgate Circus. Houses are on sale from £595 and *The Count of Monte Cristo* is showing at the Palmadium. We are looking down Chase Road, with the old Bell Inn on the left of the picture.

This scene in Chase Side, 1930, has been completely transformed. The entrance to James Howarth's premises on the extreme left still exists, but the cottages have been replaced by shops.

The villagers turn out in 1901, to wish Sir Thomas Lipton *bon voyage* on his departure to compete for the Americas Cup in *Shamrock II*. Note the Crown Hotel, on the extreme right, and the absence of traffic.

The site of Enfield West Tube Station in 1930, on the corner of Bramley Road and Chase Road. The station duly opened in 1933, and was officially renamed Oakwood in 1946.

Looking from The Bourne towards what is now Southgate Circus, December 1926. The shops in the far distance were soon to be demolished to make way for the Tube station. The boundary wall of the Queen Elizabeth Lodge estate is visible on the right of the picture.

Bourneside, home of John Miles, JP, long-time resident, and, like his neighbour John Bradshaw, highly respected and revered by the villagers for his good work in public life. A very successful businessman, he died in 1921.

It is the Saturday morning picture show at the Odeon, the much-loved cinema in The Bourne, which opened in 1931. After some intermittent closures and renaming, the final demise came in January 1981.

Grovelands, home of the Taylor family, which served as a military hospital during the First World War. The house, built by Walker Gray in 1797, was designed by John Nash. It now provides sixty-five beds for patients suffering short-term mental and other related problems.

Work goes ahead on the construction of a new road, Queen Elizabeth Drive, through the beautifully wooded grounds of the Grovelands estate.

Blagdens Lane, once called Zion Lane, is named after Robert Blagden, who ran a school called the Zion House Academy on the corner of the lane and High Street. It remained a quiet backwater well into modern times, a peaceful reminder of the past.

The history of Southgate Cycling Club goes back to 1886; this picture shows the annual sports meeting of 1888 in progress on Chapel Fields. The names of the competitors and their 'assists' include many local favourites and, through the trees, we catch a glimpse of Christ Church.

Arnos Grove, 1890, home of the Walker family, with commanding views overlooking the Pymmes Brook valley and beyond. The entrance portico, pictured here, was demolished in 1935, when 'Northmet' built the new north wing.

The magnificent entrance hall and staircase of Arnos Grove, still evident today, features murals and ceiling decoration created in 1723 by the fine Italian artist, Gerrard Lanscroon.

The Cherry Tree. Post coaches used to call here regularly on their way north. Parts of the building date back to the sixteenth century, and a small village community, once named South Street, grew up around the inn.

The Duchess Pond on The Green was named after the Duchess of Chandos, who lived in the great house called Minchenden overlooking this scene. In 1928 the pond was filled in.

The village school, built by the Walkers in 1812 and demolished in 1926, was situated where Wilmer Way now joins Powys Lane. This simple single-storey building sufficed until 1886, when a new school in Chase Road replaced it.

Preparations for the extension of the Tube, in 1931, involved the skilful construction of a series of viaduct arches, to take the line across the Pymmes Brook valley in Arnos Park.

Standard Telephone & Cables of New Southgate was a major employer in the area over a long period. The company grew rapidly in the 1930s and was honoured by a visit from the President of the Industrial Welfare Society, the Duke of York (later to become King George VI) on 8 February 1935. He planted a flowering cherry and received two ivory and gold plated telephones for his daughters.

PALMERS GREEN

The village stores, on the corner of Green Lanes and Hazelwood Lane, was the centre of the old village. The lane was no more than a track, lined by a few clapboarded cottages and a tiny chapel, leading down to Hazelwood Farm, on the banks of the New River.

Ye Olde Thatched Cottage, demolished in 1938, was one of the great survivors of the old days. Built
c. 1790 as a lodge, it served as Percy Whellock's florist's and nursery in its latter years and had a unique
appeal for overseas visitors.

Hazelwood Lane, 1928. With the property development and the arrival of the motor car, a bridge was
built across the New River, and the open countryside was just a memory.

In 1890 Hazelwood Lane was just a track for the horses and carts to trundle down to the farm, or a footpath down which the villagers could stroll and admire the scenery.

The Skinners Almshouses in Fox Lane were built in 1894 in a most attractive style, with spacious lawns and gardens. They served their purpose well until ravaged by fire in January 1966, when the site was redeveloped.

The Woodman was built in 1727 as a modest cottage in a quiet country lane. In 1868 Henry Wale, a retired police sergeant, was granted a licence to serve ale in his front room, and the inn was born. It survives to this day in much altered surroundings with a modern restaurant annexe and other 'improvements'.

Broomfield Farm was situated in Powys Lane, near the pond which is now a triangle of green. It was a dairy farm, run in its latter years by Jabez Hampton, with lush pastureland all around. It was demolished in 1912 to make way for housing.

Huxley Farm in Hedge Lane comprised some 350 acres and survived into living memory, yielding to the developers in 1931. This photograph of the farmhouse was taken in May 1929.

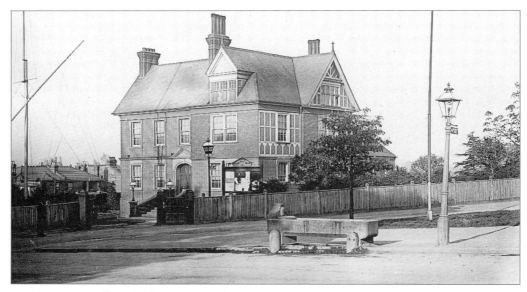

Southgate Town Hall was built in 1893 in what was a turnip field. Designed by A.R. Barker, the building had the homely appearance of a large private house. In 1914, extensive alterations and additions were made to meet the administration's growing demands.

The Triangle in the 1950s. Note the trolleybus wires and Evans & Davies, the premier store. Palmers Green was known for its high-quality and fine choice of shops through many decades, and the subsequent decline has been typical of many other areas.

The Palmadium Cinema, remembered with much affection. It opened on Christmas Eve 1920, then described as 'London's most magnificent picture house'. It served also as a theatre in its early days and was renamed the Gaumont prior to closure in February 1961.

Green Lanes showing the fine array of shops still present in 1958. Note the trolleybus wires overhead and the Palmadium on the right; note, too, the familiar Bourlet clock and the comparative lack of traffic.

Before the North Circular Road was built, Tile Kiln Lane was an important link connecting this part of the parish with Edmonton. This delightful scene shows the ford in the lane with the adjacent footbridge.

The derelict site of Bowes Manor in 1899, just prior to redevelopment. The last two owners of this once grand estate were Lord Truro, a notable lawyer and parliamentarian, and Alderman Sydney.

The old toll-gate of Tile Kiln Lane, the last to survive in North London, finally disappeared in 1927. The scale of charges ranged from one penny (animals and cyclists) to threepence for motor vehicles.

Bowes Park Methodist Church was built in 1905 with the development of the Bowes Manor estate nearby. It amalgamated with the original parent church in 1969 to become Trinity-at-Bowes, and was rebuilt two years later in more modern style.

A lovely scene in 1897, showing the ford in Powys Lane, looking towards Bowes Road, with farmland all around. The watercourse, Pymmes Brook, is now covered by a road bridge, and the whole area has been developed.

Some things never change, with key matches in progress on the greens in Broomfield Park, the home of Southgate Bowling Club. The yachting pond and mature trees can be seen in the distance.

Broomfield House in all its glory, prior to the fire of 1984. It became a focal point in the park and housed a museum and exhibition rooms. The last private resident was Sir Ralph Littler who lived there before Broomfield Park officially opened on 25 April 1903. What does the future hold? There are suggestions it may become the site of a Whitbread's restaurant.

The Garden of Remembrance in Broomfield Park includes this cairn, made with 527 stones, each representing a life laid down by residents in the First World War. The memorial has since been extended to cover the Second World War, and the names are suitably recorded.

WINCHMORE HILL

Church Hill, c. 1900. This is a lovely scene looking towards Chase Side Tavern. There are a few clapboarded cottages on the left, but it is still undeveloped on the right, and people could walk in the middle of the road unhindered by traffic.

The view looking north towards Wood Corner on Winchmore Hill Green, *c.* 1890. This footpath through the woods has now become Broad Walk.

Winchmore Hill Green, the centre of the old village. In the distance we can see the Kings Head. In the foreground, right, near the horse trough, the sign on the lamp-post reads 'Stand for Hackney Carriages'.

The owner of the horse and cart looks very relaxed as his trusty partner takes liquid refreshment on The Green. The motor car behind seems quite out of place.

A view of the fountain on Winchmore Hill Green, *c.* 1910. In the distance is the footpath entrance to the woods (now Broad Walk), with old Tidey's Corner and Hoppers Road to the left.

Close-up of Mummery's Shop, *c.* 1900, once Udall & Childs. This is a very historic part of the old village, with the entrance to Winchmore Hill Woods to the left of the picture.

The old bakehouse ovens of Chalkley's Bakery in Hoppers Road ceased to operate from about 1945, though their corner shop, in the far distance, continued to trade into the 1960s.

This rare postcard scene, looking up the hill, shows the old Queens Head inn projecting into a very narrow Station Road, with no sign of traffic. The card is dated 1914.

Rose Cottage in Vicars Moor Lane, home of Thomas Hood (1799–1845), poet and humorist of Scottish descent, who left the district after disagreeing with his landlord about repairs. The house was demolished following bomb damage during the Second World War.

Beaumont Lodge, once the home of John Wade, who gave his name to the hill. After his death in 1865, it later became Avondale College for Girls, before its demise in 1929, when the whole area was being rapidly developed.

Stonehall's herd of Jersey cattle enjoying the lush pasture and fine scenery on the large estate, situated just off Church Hill. This picture reminds us that farming once played a major role in the life of the village.

Looking up Winchmore Hill Road towards Southgate from the Chase Side Tavern. All the land on the left, once owned by the Taylors, is up for sale and development, which followed in the early 1930s.

The Retreat, an old beer house, was situated just off the Hagfields footpath (now Green Moor Link), near the junction with Dog Kennel Lane (now Green Dragon Lane). This copy of an old painting is dated 1860.

We are looking north from the railway embankment across Green Dragon Lane to Filcap's Farm, which was situated where Landra Gardens joins today. Grange Park Station did not open until 1910, when development began.

A typical scene in Grange Park early this century. Before the development, there was a delightful walk from Green Dragon Lane to Enfield along a footpath through orchards, farmland and beautiful countryside, roughly on the route now taken by Old Park Ridings and Old Park Avenue.

This photograph is dated 1935, when Southgate was an Urban District Council, and the 'dust destructor' and the swimming baths stood side by side in Barrowell Green.

Barrowell Green Baths opened in 1913, following the banning of public bathing in Broomfield Park lakes. This picture evokes so many happy memories, and so many regrets at its closure in 1983.

Pickering's Cottage, 1926. It was demolished in 1932/3, when the new Firs Lane estate was being developed. The old cottage was replaced by 83 Farm Road (on the corner of Farm Road and Laburnum Grove), once the family home of the author.

Fords Grove, looking east towards Edmonton. The Paulin Cricket Ground is today left of picture and Mortiboy's Farm has long since made way for houses.

Thanks to the wisdom of past councillors, who ensured the creation of our local parks, we can still enjoy a stroll around the lake in Grovelands, away from the noise of busy suburban streets.

TRANSPORT

In 1849, Eastern Counties Railway, later to become the Great Eastern Railway, opened a branch line from Water Lane (Angel Road) to Enfield Town, where a former private school in Southbury Road was converted to serve as the railway station.

Percy Whellock's entry in the Regents Park Parade of 1929. Percy was a well-known nurseryman and florist, whose business at Ye Olde Thatched Cottage, in Palmers Green, was familiar to locals and tourists alike.

Enfield Chase Station, Great Northern Railway, in Windmill Hill. The building became obsolete in 1910, when a new station was opened further down the hill. This enabled a bridge to be built above the roadway when the line was extended out to Cuffley.

The 'rush hour' at Palmers Green Station, which opened in 1871. The horsebus and a private carriage have delivered their passengers who will continue their journey by rail into town.

This is not a local horsebus, but a close-up of this once very important part of our transport system is included to illustrate how different things were before mechanization.

Life was so much slower in the days of the horsetrams, seen here at Tramway Avenue in Edmonton.

The same location as above, with a close-up of the service operating through Edmonton, Tottenham and Seven Sisters to Finsbury Park.

A very pristine looking, but rather deserted, Ponders End Station, Great Eastern Railway.

Hadley North Tunnel, South Portal, July 1958, showing a late stage in the construction of a new tunnel to facilitate line widening.

Work in progress at Wood Green, in 1904, to extend the tramway northwards, from Manor House as far as Enfield Town. The amount of labour required for this huge project is evident.

The same scene as above with the trams now operating. The tramway reached the Green Dragon, Winchmore Hill, by 1907, and Enfield Town by 1909.

Work on the tramway continues in London Road, Enfield.

The final work on the tramway being carried out at the end of the line, outside the George Inn. Two of the local lads are checking on progress.

The first tram arrives, and the workmen take a well-earned rest. The Nags Head, in the background, has gone and the corner has been completely redeveloped incorporating the Pizza Hut restaurant.

Scenes of celebration as the first tramcar to Enfield Wash arrives with senior officials on board, 11 December 1907.

The trams in their heyday, all clean and shiny, in Southbury Road, 1935.

The motor buses reached Southgate in 1912, the familiar No. 29 being depicted here at The Cherry Tree.

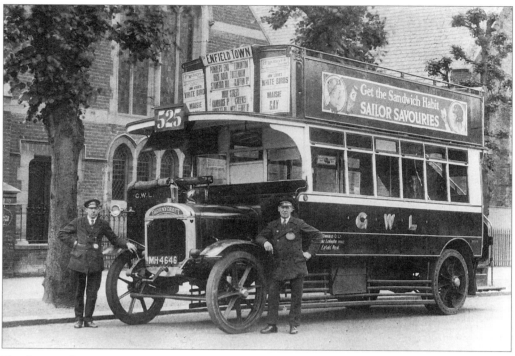

The driver and conductor on the 525 to Enfield Town take a breather. Note the solid tyres and open top deck.

The trolleybuses had many blessings. They were fast, quiet and environment-friendly. They replaced many of the old tram routes, but were phased out in the early 1960s.

The huge bus garage in Tramway Avenue, which was eventually demolished in 1986.

Tunnelling work in progress on the Piccadilly Line in 1931, near to Southgate Station which opened in March 1933. The extension from Finsbury Park terminated at Cockfosters and prompted rapid development in all the areas affected.

Eastpole Farm in Bramley Road, situated opposite the junction of Chase Road, 1931. It was soon to be lost to make way for the Tube. The site of Enfield West Station can be seen on the right, later to be renamed Oakwood.

Apart from a short distance either side of Southgate Station, the Tube is mostly on the surface in this area.

The site of Arnos Grove Station in 1930/31. Note the open countryside of the old Arnos Grove estate and the spire of Christ Church in the distance, extreme right.

The classic lines of Arnos Grove Station. The Piccadilly Line extension from Finsbury Park to Arnos Grove opened in 1932.

A series of viaduct arches carry the Tube tracks across the Pymmes Brook valley in Arnos Park, and we are still able to witness today a fine example of the bricklayers' skills of the 1930s.

WARTIME

With the threat of war came the setting up of Air Raid Precautions (ARP) with a network of warden's posts.
This one is thought to have been in Town Park.

There were many campaigns urging the public to invest in National Savings and thus help the war effort, and parades were organized to help publicize these events. These photographs show the 'Wings for Victory' campaign in 1943. The 30th battalion, Middlesex Home Guard, sets off from Eastfield Road (above), passing the saluting base in Enfield Town (below).

A member of the Home Guard, which was formed to combat the threat of invasion. Notwithstanding the affectionate tag of 'Dad's Army', their contribution was of real value to the war effort.

The 25th battalion, Middlesex Home Guard, at Elmscott in Bush Hill.

Clearing up in London Road, Enfield, from landmine damage in November 1940.

Serious damage caused by high explosive (HE) bombs in Chapel Street, Enfield, 11 April 1941. The Anderson shelter proved resilient to all but the direct hit.

The onslaught resumed in 1944–5 with the V1 flying bombs and V2 rockets. This picture shows the 'doodlebug' damage in Marrilyne Avenue, Brimsdown, July 1944.

The morning after another night of destruction in Osidge Lane, Southgate.

A scene of devastation in Hampden Way, Southgate, with loss of life and extensive damage to property.

Edmonton residents clear up the debris in November 1943, after German raids.

The Alcazar Cinema in Fore Street, Edmonton, and the adjoining dance hall were completely wrecked by HE bombs in the air raid of 23 August 1940.

The Alcazar had opened in June 1913, with rebuilding work carried out in 1933, following the arrival of the 'talkies'. Now it lay in ruins.

This incident in Green Lanes, opposite the Capitol Cinema, is clearly remembered by the author. There was severe damage, and a fractured gas main posed a threat. All has been rebuilt and you have to look hard now to 'see the joins'.

Serious damage to the bungalows in Links Rise, Slades Hill.

Saturday 15 March 1941. A very sad night for Palmers Green, when a stick of three bombs fell near the junction of Bowes Road and Green Lanes, with direct hits on Princes Dance Hall, a bus and Barclays Bank (seen here), resulting in extensive damage and many casualties.

The gruesome task of clearing up goes on in Oakwood Park Road.

Further serious damage in London Road, Enfield, at the height of the blitz.

The blast from a landmine, dropped by parachute, caused widespread damage, as seen here in Willow Road, Enfield.

Devastation in Anglesey Road, Ponders End, as two officials check the crater.

The air raids in 1941 were sporadic, but nevertheless caused extensive damage to life and property, as witness this scene in Nightingale Road, Edmonton, on 20 March 1941.

Captain William Leefe Robinson VC was one of the great heroes of the First World War. He will always be associated with the shooting down of a zeppelin in the early hours of Sunday 3 September 1916. The airship SL 11 had dropped bombs on the eastern side of the borough before meeting its fate. Thousands of people made the pilgrimage to nearby Cuffley to see the remains, search for souvenirs and pay tribute to the courage of this man. Robinson was later posted to the Western Front where he was captured and taken prisoner on 5 April 1917. Cruelly treated in a succession of PoW camps, his health deteriorated and he died, aged twenty-three, just seventeen days after repatriation.

INDEX

Aldermans Hill 133
Angel Road 74, 89
Anglesey Road 156
Arnos Grove 102, 103
Arnos Park 105, 144
ARP 145
Baker Street 44, 45
Barges 72
Barrowell Green 128
Beech Hill 14
Blagdens Lane 101
Botany Bay 12
Bourne, The 98, 99
Bourne Hill 110
Bowes Manor 114
Bowes Road 116, 143
Bramley Road 98, 142
Bridge Road 82
Broad Walk 120
Broomfield House 117
Broomfield Park 117, 118
Bulls Cross 19
Bury Street West 50, 51, 52, 53
Buses 139, 140
Bush Hill 48
Bush Hill Park Golf Club 48
Cannon Hill 102, 103
Capel Manor 24
Cecil Road 34
Chalk Lane 10
Chapel Fields 102
Chapel Street 149
Chase Road, Southgate 98
Chase Side, Enfield 39, 41, 42
Chase Side, Southgate 97
Cherry Tree, The 104, 139
Church Hill 119
Church Street Edmonton 83, 84,
    85, 86
Church Street Enfield 25, 27, 32,
    33, 34, 35, 36
Clay Hill 7, 11, 13
Cooks Hole Road 8
Duchess Pond 104
Edmonton Green 77, 78, 79, 80
Enfield Lock 57, 73, 75
Enfield Wash 60, 138
Farm Road 129

Fords Grove 129
Fore Street 81, 82, 87, 88, 89, 90,
    151, 152
Forty Hall 15, 20, 21, 22, 23
Forty Hill 16, 17, 18
Fox Lane 110
Gentlemans Row 37, 40
Goat Lane 16, 18
Government Row 57
Green, The W.H. 121, 122
Green Dragon Lane 126
Green Lanes N13 107, 108, 112,
    113, 154
Green Lanes N21 153
Green Moor Link 126
Grovelands 100, 130
Hadley Tunnel 135
Hampden Way 150
Ha'penny Bridge 75
Hazelwood Lane 107, 108, 109
Hedge Lane 111
Hertford Road 58, 60, 61, 68, 78,
    81
High Road, Wood Green 136
High Street, Ponders End 63, 66,
    67, 68, 70
High Street, Southgate 95
Home Guard 147, 148
Hoppers Road 123
Horse and Cart 132
Horsebuses 133
Horsetrams 134
Jews Corner 49
Langhedge Lane 89
Lea Valley Viaduct 74, 91
Lincoln Road 62
Links Rise 153
Little Bury Street 49, 50, 52
London Road, 26, 137, 148,
    155
M25 14
Maidens Bridge 24
Market Place, Enfield 30, 31, 32
Marrilyne Avenue 149
Nightingale Road, Edmonton 156
North Middlesex Hospital 94
Oakwood Park Road 154
Old Forge Road 19

Old Park Avenue 39, 127
Old Park Ridings 127
Old Park Road 38
Ordnance Road 58
Osidge Lane 150
Parades 146
Park Avenue 54
Parsonage Lane 41
Phipps Hatch Lane 9
Picketts Lock 76
Ponders End Lock 71, 72
Powys Lane 105, 111, 116
Pymmes Park 92
Queen Anne's Gardens 47
Queen Elizabeth Drive 100
Railways 131, 132, 133, 135
Rammey Marsh Lock 76
Ridgeway, The 10
Robinson VC, Capt. W.L. 157
Rosebery Road 86
Royal Small Arms 55, 56
Silver Street, Edmonton 93
Silver Street, Enfield 42, 43, 46
Slades Hill 43
South Street 64, 65, 67, 69,
    135
Southbury Road 131, 139
Southgate Circus 96, 98
Standard Telephones 106
Station Road 123
Stonehall 125
Tile Kiln Lane 114, 115
Town, The 28, 29, 30, 137, 138
Trams 136, 137, 138, 139
Tramway Avenue 134, 141
Trent Park 12
Trolleybuses 140, 141
Tube 141, 142, 143, 144
Turkey Street 59, 62
Vicars Moor Lane 124
Village Road 54
Wades Hill 124
Weir Hall 94
Whitewebbs Lane 8, 11
Willow Road 155
Winchmore Hill Road 125
Windmill Hill 38, 132
Wright's Mill 68

BRITAIN IN OLD PHOTOGRAPHS

Aberystwyth & North Ceredigion
Around Abingdon
Acton
Alderney: A Second Selection
Along the Avon from Stratford to
  Tewkesbury
Altrincham
Amersham
Around Amesbury
Anglesey
Arnold & Bestwood
Arnold & Bestwood: A Second
  Selection
Arundel & the Arun Valley
Ashbourne
Around Ashby-de-la-Zouch
Avro Aircraft
Aylesbury
Balham & Tooting
Banburyshire
Barnes, Mortlake & Sheen
Barnsley
Bath
Beaconsfield
Bedford
Bedfordshire at Work
Bedworth
Beverley
Bexley
Bideford
Bilston
Birmingham Railways
Bishop's Stortford &
  Sawbridgeworth
Bishopstone & Seaford
Bishopstone & Seaford: A Second
  Selection
Black Country Aviation
Black Country Railways
Black Country Road Transport
Blackburn
Blackpool
Around Blandford Forum
Bletchley
Bolton
Bournemouth
Bradford
Braintree & Bocking at Work
Brecon
Brentwood
Bridgwater & the River Parrett
Bridlington
Bridport & the Bride Valley
Brierley Hill
Brighton & Hove
Brighton & Hove: A Second
  Selection
Bristol
Around Bristol
Brixton & Norwood
Early Broadstairs & St Peters
Bromley, Keston & Hayes

Buckingham & District
Burford
Bury
Bushbury
Camberwell
Cambridge
Cannock Yesterday & Today
Canterbury: A Second Selection
Castle Combe to Malmesbury
Chadwell Heath
Chard & Ilminster
Chatham Dockyard
Chatham & Gillingham
Cheadle
Cheam & Belmont
Chelmsford
Cheltenham: A Second Selection
Cheltenham at War
Cheltenham in the 1950s
Chepstow & the River Wye
Chesham Yesterday & Today
Cheshire Railways
Chester
Chippenham & Lacock
Chiswick
Chorley & District
Cirencester
Around Cirencester
Clacton-on-Sea
Around Clitheroe
Clwyd Railways
Clydesdale
Colchester
Colchester 1940–70
Colyton & Seaton
The Cornish Coast
Corsham & Box
The North Cotswolds
Coventry: A Second Selection
Around Coventry
Cowes & East Cowes
Crawley New Town
Around Crawley
Crewkerne & the Ham Stone
  Villages
Cromer
Croydon
Crystal Palace, Penge & Anerley
Darlington
Darlington: A Second Selection
Dawlish & Teignmouth
Deal
Derby
Around Devizes
Devon Aerodromes
East Devon at War
Around Didcot & the Hagbournes
Dorchester
Douglas
Dumfries
Dundee at Work
Durham People

Durham at Work
Ealing & Northfields
East Grinstead
East Ham
Eastbourne
Elgin
Eltham
Ely
Enfield
Around Epsom
Esher
Evesham to Bredon
Exeter
Exmouth & Budleigh Salterton
Fairey Aircraft
Falmouth
Farnborough
Farnham: A Second Selection
Fleetwood
Folkestone: A Second Selection
Folkestone: A Third Selection
The Forest of Dean
Frome
Fulham
Galashiels
Garsington
Around Garstang
Around Gillingham
Gloucester
Gloucester: from the Walwin
  Collection
North Gloucestershire at War
South Gloucestershire at War
Gosport
Goudhurst to Tenterden
Grantham
Gravesend
Around Gravesham
Around Grays
Great Yarmouth
Great Yarmouth: A Second
  Selection
Greenwich & Woolwich
Grimsby
Around Grimsby
Grimsby Docks
Gwynedd Railways
Hackney: A Second Selection
Hackney: A Third Selection
From Haldon to Mid-Dartmoor
Hammersmith & Shepherds Bush
Hampstead to Primrose Hill
Harrow & Pinner
Hastings
Hastings: A Second Selection
Haverfordwest
Hayes & West Drayton
Around Haywards Heath
Around Heathfield
Around Heathfield: A Second
  Selection
Around Helston

Around Henley-on-Thames
Herefordshire
Herne Bay
Heywood
The High Weald
The High Weald: A Second
  Selection
Around Highworth
Around Highworth & Faringdon
Hitchin
Holderness
Honiton & the Otter Valley
Horsham & District
Houghton-le-Spring &
  Hetton-le-Hole
Houghton-le-Spring & Hetton-le-
  Hole: A Second Selection
Huddersfield: A Second Selection
Huddersfield: A Third Selection
Ilford
Ilfracombe
Ipswich: A Second Selection
Islington
Jersey: A Third Selection
Kendal
Kensington & Chelsea
East Kent at War
Keswick & the Central Lakes
Around Keynsham & Saltford
The Changing Face of Keynsham
Kingsbridge
Kingston
Kinver
Kirkby & District
Kirkby Lonsdale
Around Kirkham
Knowle & Dorridge
The Lake Counties at Work
Lancashire
The Lancashire Coast
Lancashire North of the Sands
Lancashire Railways
East Lancashire at War
Around Lancaster
Lancing & Sompting
Around Leamington Spa
Around Leamington Spa:
  A Second Selection
Leeds in the News
Leeds Road & Rail
Around Leek
Leicester
The Changing Face of Leicester
Leicester at Work
Leicestershire People
Around Leighton Buzzard &
  Linslade
Letchworth
Lewes
Lewisham & Deptford:
  A Second Selection
Lichfield

Lincoln	Penwith	Smethwick	Tunbridge Wells: A Second
Lincoln Cathedral	Penzance & Newlyn	Somerton & Langport	Selection
The Lincolnshire Coast	Around Pershore	Southampton	Twickenham
Liverpool	Around Plymouth	Southend-on-Sea	Uley, Dursley & Cam
Around Llandudno	Poole	Southport	The Upper Fal
Around Lochaber	Portsmouth	Southwark	The Upper Tywi Valley
Theatrical London	Poulton-le-Fylde	Southwell	Uxbridge, Hillingdon & Cowley
Around Louth	Preston	Southwold to Aldeburgh	The Vale of Belvoir
The Lower Fal Estuary	Prestwich	Stafford	The Vale of Conway
Lowestoft	Pudsey	Around Stafford	Ventnor
Luton	Radcliffe	Staffordshire Railways	Wakefield
Lympne Airfield	RAF Chivenor	Around Staveley	Wallingford
Lytham St Annes	RAF Cosford	Stepney	Walsall
Maidenhead	RAF Hawkinge	Stevenage	Waltham Abbey
Around Maidenhead	RAF Manston	The History of Stilton Cheese	Wandsworth at War
Around Malvern	RAF Manston: A Second Selection	Stoke-on-Trent	Wantage, Faringdon & the Vale
Manchester	RAF St Mawgan	Stoke Newington	Villages
Manchester Road & Rail	RAF Tangmere	Stonehouse to Painswick	Around Warwick
Mansfield	Ramsgate & Thanet Life	Around Stony Stratford	Weardale
Marlborough: A Second Selection	Reading	Around Stony Stratford: A Second	Weardale: A Second Selection
Marylebone & Paddington	Reading: A Second Selection	Selection	Wednesbury
Around Matlock	Redditch & the Needle District	Stowmarket	Wells
Melton Mowbray	Redditch: A Second Selection	Streatham	Welshpool
Around Melksham	Richmond, Surrey	Stroud & the Five Valleys	West Bromwich
The Mendips	Rickmansworth	Stroud & the Five Valleys: A	West Wight
Merton & Morden	Around Ripley	Second Selection	Weston-super-Mare
Middlesbrough	The River Soar	Stroud's Golden Valley	Around Weston-super-Mare
Midsomer Norton & Radstock	Romney Marsh	The Stroudwater and Thames &	Weymouth & Portland
Around Mildenhall	Romney Marsh: A Second	Severn Canals	Around Wheatley
Milton Keynes	Selection	The Stroudwater and Thames &	Around Whetstone
Minehead	Rossendale	Severn Canals: A Second	Whitchurch to Market Drayton
Monmouth & the River Wye	Around Rotherham	Selection	Around Whitstable
The Nadder Valley	Rugby	Suffolk at Work	Wigton & the Solway Plain
Newark	Around Rugeley	Suffolk at Work: A Second	Willesden
Around Newark	Ruislip	Selection	Around Wilton
Newbury	Around Ryde	The Heart of Suffolk	Wimbledon
Newport, Isle of Wight	St Albans	Sunderland	Around Windsor
The Norfolk Broads	St Andrews	Sutton	Wingham, Addisham &
Norfolk at War	Salford	Swansea	Littlebourne
North Fylde	Salisbury	Swindon: A Third Selection	Wisbech
North Lambeth	Salisbury: A Second Selection	Swindon: A Fifth Selection	Witham & District
North Walsham & District	Salisbury: A Third Selection	Around Tamworth	Witney
Northallerton	Around Salisbury	Taunton	Around Witney
Northampton	Sandhurst & Crowthorne	Around Taunton	The Witney District
Around Norwich	Sandown & Shanklin	Teesdale	Wokingham
Nottingham 1944–74	Sandwich	Teesdale: A Second Selection	Around Woodbridge
The Changing Face of Nottingham	Scarborough	Tenbury Wells	Around Woodstock
Victorian Nottingham	Scunthorpe	Around Tettenhall & Codshall	Woolwich
Nottingham Yesterday & Today	Seaton, Lyme Regis & Axminster	Tewkesbury & the Vale of	Woolwich Royal Arsenal
Nuneaton	Around Seaton & Sidmouth	Gloucester	Around Wootton Bassett,
Around Oakham	Sedgley & District	Thame to Watlington	Cricklade & Purton
Ormskirk & District	The Severn Vale	Around Thatcham	Worcester
Otley & District	Sherwood Forest	Around Thirsk	Worcester in a Day
Oxford: The University	Shrewsbury	Thornbury to Berkeley	Around Worcester
Oxford Yesterday & Today	Shrewsbury: A Second Selection	Tipton	Worcestershire at Work
Oxfordshire Railways: A Second	Shropshire Railways	Around Tonbridge	Around Worthing
Selection	Skegness	Trowbridge	Wotton-under-Edge to Chipping
Oxfordshire at School	Around Skegness	Around Truro	Sodbury
Around Padstow	Skipton & the Dales	TT Races	Wymondham & Attleborough
Pattingham & Wombourne	Around Slough	Tunbridge Wells	The Yorkshire Wolds

To order any of these titles please telephone our distributor, Littlehampton Book Services on 01903 721596
For a catalogue of these and our other titles please ring Regina Schinner on 01453 731114